PREPARE FOR AN OUTPOURING
OF GRACE UPON YOUR LIFE

Mary's Mantle Consecration Prayer Journal is a companion book to be used in tandem with *Mary's Mantle Consecration: A Spiritual Retreat for Heaven's Help*—a self-guided retreat that has resulted in miracles in the lives and hearts of those who have applied themselves to it. This prayer journal, an added bonus to the program of consecration, will take you even deeper into your soul and into God's transforming grace.

Both *Mary's Mantle Consecration Prayer Journal* and
Mary's Mantle Consecration: A Spiritual Retreat for Heaven's Help
Are available in Spanish/Están disponibles en español

Available through www.QueenofPeaceMedia.com
See **www.MarysMantleConsecration.com**

To learn more, watch the videos, or order the poster and coloring page that accompany *Mary's Mantle Consecration*, go to www.MarysMantleConsecration.com.

Queen of Peace Media:

books, videos, blogs, prayer requests, and more, that help you nurture your faith and *Find your way Home.*

Go to www.QueenofPeaceMedia.com.
Sign up for our newsletter to be updated with our new content.

RADIO MARIA SHOW
"Find Your Way Home"

with Christine Watkins and Christine Bacon

Tune into Christine Watkins' live weekly show, Thursdays from 7 to 8 p.m., PST, also posted on Queen of Peace Media's YouTube and Rumble channels. On www.Rumble.com, go to www.rumble.com/user/QueenofPeaceMedia. To watch or be notified of our new YouTube videos, see www.youtube.com/c/QueenofPeaceMedia and click "Subscribe" and the bell icon (top right of the screen). Also go to www.queenofpeacemedia.com/home.

Visit Us on Social Media—Subscribe, Like, and Follow us!

At www.YouTube.com, search for Queen of Peace Media
Rumble: www.rumble.com/user/QueenofPeaceMedia
Facebook: www.facebook.com/QueenofPeaceMedia
MeWe: www.mewe.com/join/queenofpeacemedia

MARY'S MANTLE CONSECRATION PRAYER JOURNAL

CHRISTINE WATKINS
&
LAURA DAYTON

A Companion Journal to

MARY'S MANTLE CONSECRATION
A SPIRITUAL RETREAT FOR HEAVEN'S HELP

Edited by William Underwood

Cover background art by Sandra Lubreto Dettori. To order prints of Dettori's work, see www.threearchangels.etsy.com.

Books may be purchased in quantity by contacting the publisher directly at orders@queenofpeacemedia.com.

ISBN-13: 978-1-947701-08-3
ISBN-10: 1-947701-08-8

CONTENTS

INTRODUCTION

Mary's Mantle Consecration Prayer Journal is a companion to the book and 46-day retreat, *Mary's Mantle Consecration: A Spiritual Retreat for Heaven's Help.* This prayer journal is for those who wish to inflame their souls with virtues and the gifts of the Holy Spirit, and who desire to love God and their neighbor more deeply. It is for those who have decided to purposefully climb the ladder that leads to their eternal home.

"The holy virtues are like the ladder of Jacob and the unholy vices are like the chains that fell off the chief apostle Peter. The virtues lead from one to another and carry heavenward the man who chooses him. Vices on the other hand beget and stifle one another."
— *St. John Climacus*

This journal guides the reader along the rungs of the ladder we all must ascend in this life, if we are to become the creatures that God intended when He first fashioned us in His heart.

"Be who God meant you to be and you will set the world on fire."
— *St. Catherine of Siena*

Each day of the retreat, sometime after you have read the day's meditation in the book, *Mary's Mantle Consecration,* you are invited to pick up this journal. It will first ask you to begin with a couple minutes of prayer. This is critical. Please quiet your spirit and take that time to communicate with God. Then the journal will ask you questions and provide insights from Scripture and the wisdom of saints to help you explore and apply the day's virtue or gift in your life. The more deeply you dive into the recesses of your soul, the more freely your spirit will rise to the heights. God is waiting. . . The work is up to you.

The importance of this inward journey of exploration and renewal on behalf of your life and the world cannot be overestimated.

"The goal of a virtuous life is to be like God."
— *St. Gregory of Nyssa*

1st Star: Thanksgiving

Remember that you are in the holy presence of God. Close your eyes and take a deep breath.
Ask God to grant you a heart that swells naturally with gratitude.

Spiritual Exercise

One of God's first acts of love for you was to create this world so that you could be born into it. He gave you His most precious possession: His Son. He has provided for you all your days. He gave you this life, this moment, this breath. Until your final heartbeat, you are free to receive His Body and His Blood, His mercy and His forgiveness—salvation.

Everything we are and all that we possess, even that which we have rightly earned, is pure gift. The only thing we can claim as our very own is our sin. Since all of the good within and around us comes from the magnanimous and benevolent hand of our Creator, take a moment to write down some of the many gifts and graces He has bestowed on you. With all that God has given and done for you, what might you wish to give to Him in thanksgiving?

"No duty is more urgent than that of returning thanks."

—*St. Ambrose*

Journaling Space

"As he continued his journey to Jerusalem, he traveled through Samaria and Galilee. As he was entering a village, ten lepers met [him]. They stood at a distance from him and raised their voice, saying, "Jesus, Master! Have pity on us!" And when he saw them, he said, "Go show yourselves to the priests." As they were going they were cleansed. And one of them, realizing he had been healed, returned, glorifying God in a loud voice; and he fell at the feet of Jesus and thanked him. He was a Samaritan. Jesus said in reply, "Ten were cleansed, were they not? Where are the other nine? Has none but this foreigner returned to give thanks to God?" Then he said to him, "Stand up and go; your faith has saved you."
——*Luke 17:11-19*

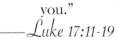

2nd Star: Commitment

Remember that you are in the holy presence of God. Close your eyes and take a deep breath. Aloud or in the silent cell of your heart, ask the Lord to lift you up where you feel most weak.

Spiritual Exercise

Contemplate an area of your life or spirit where you stumble easily, where you are prone to failure, and perhaps fall, time and again. In your mind's eye, see your Father in heaven extending His merciful hand toward you, and with tender, paternal love, lifting you into His palm. Sense Him gently dusting you off and encouraging you to try again. Imagine Him cheering for you, His child, with His full support: "You can do this! Don't give up! Have faith. I am with you. Just try."

In what ways are you aware of God's guiding hand in your life?

"God does not require us to succeed; He only requires that you try."

—St. Mother Teresa

Journaling Space

"Do you not know? Have you not heard? The LORD is God from of old, creator of the ends of the earth. He does not faint or grow weary, and his knowledge is beyond scrutiny. He gives power to the faint, abundant strength to the weak. Though young men faint and grow weary, and youths stagger and fall, they that hope in the LORD will renew their strength, they will soar on eagles' wings; they will run and not grow weary, walk and not grow faint."

Isaiah 40:28-31

3rd Star: Love

Remember that you are in the holy presence of God. Close your eyes and take a deep breath.
Ask Mary to show you how to love as she loves.

Spiritual Exercise

Love costs, and love of Jesus and our neighbor costs a great deal. How have you experienced this truth in your own life? Is there a cross of love you must carry whose weight cuts into your shoulders, deeper than you feel you can bear? Have you thrown this cross to the ground in bitterness and defeat, only to be forced to retrieve it again? Ask Mother Mary to make it lighter in the manner of Simon of Cyrene. Just as Simon was moved to help bear Jesus' load, so too will Mary come to your aid. The heaviest end of the cross will no longer be yours to carry. When you look up, you will see your Mother shouldering it for you.

In what ways is God asking you to be like Mary and help carry the crosses that weigh heavily on others?

"Where there is no love, put love, and you will draw out love."

—St. John of the Cross

Journaling Space

"As the Father loves me, so I also love you. Remain in my love. If you keep my commandments, you will remain in my love, just as I have kept my Father's commandments and remain in his love. I have told you this so that my joy may be in you and your joy may be complete. This is my commandment: love one another as I love you. No one has greater love than this, to lay down one's life for one's friends."

—*John 15:9-13*

4th Star: Trust

Remember that you are in the holy presence of God. Close your eyes and take a deep breath. Say the words, "Jesus, I trust in you," and allow them to fill your soul with peace and serenity.

Spiritual Exercise

Is there anything the Lord, Jesus Christ, would refuse to suffer, if He knew it would help you? Jesus profoundly grieves when one of His own is critically wounded; He aches when you are hurt, even in the slightest way; and He mixes His tears with yours so that not a drop of your shared suffering should be wasted.

This same Man holds the world in His hands. He commands the stars to move and the sea to calm. Is there anything outside of His control? Is it possible that the struggle you are facing is too unmanageable for Him? No!

In everything Jesus Christ wills or permits in your life, His ultimate plan is nothing less than to carry you in His arms to heaven, where He will free you from all suffering and wipe away your every tear—forever. If this is His goal with you, and if there is nothing He cannot do, is there something still keeping you from placing your full trust in Him?

"Now I really rejoice when something does not go as I wish— because I see that He wants our trust—that is why in the loss let us praise God as if we have got everything."
—St. Mother Teresa

Journaling Space

"Blessed are those who trust in the **LORD**; the **LORD** will be their trust. They are like a tree planted beside the waters that stretches out its roots to the stream: It does not fear heat when it comes, its leaves stay green; In the year of drought it shows no distress, but still produces fruit."

—*Jeremiah 17:7-8*

5th Star: Generosity

Remember that you are in the holy presence of God. Close your eyes and take a deep breath. Ask God to free your heart from any fear of not having enough, of not having what you need.

Spiritual Exercise

Imagine yourself at the end of your life. All that you possessed—your money, your things—is gone. Everything has evaporated into dust, and you remain with only your soul, bare before Jesus. In this moment, your spirit understands, in a profound and completely new way, that you can only keep what you gave away.

Think now of a person, a cause, a project, or a ministry, something that you've felt inspired or nudged to support generously, but you questioned the impulse or retracted it. If you are unaccustomed to praying and asking God how *He* would like you to allocate your resources and time, especially to the less fortunate, you must know that to give in this way is a calling for each Christian. It isn't an arbitrary choice for those who wish to live in the Kingdom; it is a prerequisite for entering.

"...for it is in giving that we receive..."
—St. Francis of Assisi

Journaling Space

"When he looked up he saw some wealthy people putting their offerings into the treasury and he noticed a poor widow putting in two small coins. He said, 'I tell you truly, this poor widow put in more than all the rest; for those others have all made offerings from their surplus wealth, but she, from her poverty, has offered her whole livelihood.'"
——*Luke 21:1-4*

6th Star: Tenacity

Remember that you are in the holy presence of God. Close your eyes and take a deep breath. Ask Mary to help you flee from distractions, however enjoyable, noble, or necessary they may seem, and to clear a path of prayer for you each day.

Spiritual Exercise

Do you find yourself setting aside time each day for prayer? If so, what is your preferred way to pray and why? If you do not normally make time for prayer each day, pinpoint for yourself the personal vulnerability or worldly attractions that remove you from conversation and communion with God.

The devil hides in our distractions. If your time in prayer is easily whisked away, then you have made something in your life more important than God. What might that be? The manner in which you spend your free time will lead you to the answer.

"Whoever flees prayer flees all that is good."
—St. John of the Cross

Journaling Space

"In all circumstances, hold faith as a shield, to quench all [the] flaming arrows of the evil one. And take the helmet of salvation and the sword of the Spirit, which is the word of God. With all prayer and supplication, pray at every opportunity in the Spirit. To that end, be watchful with all perseverance and supplication for all the holy ones."

—*Ephesians 6:6-18*

7th Star: Endurance

Remember that you are in the holy presence of God. Close your eyes and take a deep breath.
Ask the Holy Spirit for spiritual tools to help you endure when your strength is waning.

Spiritual Exercise

Reflect on all the moments of crisis in your life when you felt like you could not endure and could not see a way out. Think of how the Lord carried you through every single one of those times, and thank Him for His care and provision. In future moments of trial, let your thoughts turn to Jesus and His endurance in the face of Calvary. Call on Mary, who did not condemn anyone or question God's will as she heard her Son's screams from the Cross, but held firm in her faith.

Ask now for Jesus and Mary to give you Their endurance when hardships strike and you approach an unknown future.

"Do not fear the conflict. Do not flee it. Where there is no struggle, there is no virtue. Where love and faith are not tempted, it is not possible to be sure whether they are really present. They are tried and revealed in adversity, in difficult and grievous circumstances."

— St. John Chrysostom

Journaling Space

"No trial has come to you but what is human. God is faithful and will not let you be tried beyond your strength; but with the trial he will also provide a way out, so that you may be able to bear it."
—1 Corinthians 10:13

8th Star: Forgiveness

Remember that you are in the holy presence of God. Close your eyes and take a deep breath. Imagine extending an olive branch of peace to someone who has wronged you.

Spiritual Exercise

Even in His last moments, Jesus forgave. Did He reserve His forgiveness for His family, His friends, those who showed Him kindness? No. He forgave the people who beat Him, insulted Him, disrobed Him, condemned Him, hung Him on a cross, and murdered Him. What does this say about our calling to forgive?

Ask the Lord to reveal to you if there are people toward whom you harbor unforgiveness. Is there someone in your own family, perhaps? A boyfriend, girlfriend or spouse from long ago? Are you refusing to forgive yourself for something in your past? Make a list. Then take a few minutes, now, to write a letter—one you will never send—to a person on your list, perhaps even yourself.

Begin with: "Dear _____, I am angry with you because..." and go into great detail. When you are done, take a deep breath and begin another letter to that same person. "Dear _____, I forgive you for..." This exercise is often hard to attempt. Don't think, just begin. Write as many letters as you need to. Your writing will help you release years of pain and experience more freedom in Christ.

"The sign of sincere love is to forgive wrongs done to us. It was with such love that the Lord loved the world."

—St. Mark the Ascetic

Journaling Space

Then Peter approaching asked him, "Lord, if my brother sins against me, how often must I forgive him? As many as seven times?" Jesus answered, "I say to you, not seven times but seventy-seven times. That is why the kingdom of heaven may be likened to a king who decided to settle accounts with his servants (. . .) His master summoned him and said to him, 'You wicked servant! I forgave you your entire debt because you begged me to. Should you not have had pity on your fellow servant, as I had pity on you?' Then in anger his master handed him over to the torturers until he should pay back the whole debt. So will my heavenly Father do to you, unless each of you forgives his brother from his heart."

——*Matthew 18:21-23;32-35*

9th Star: Perseverance

Remember that you are in the holy presence of God. Close your eyes and take a deep breath. Call out to Jesus in prayer, "Teach me how to persevere in this life to arrive one day within Heaven's gates that I may rest in Your arms forever."

Spiritual Exercise

Countless times in your past, you have hoped beyond sight, worked without reward, and loved without success. Yet you have persevered. There is only one thing that can stop you from reaching the goal of sainthood, which Christ has chosen for you. That one thing is you. Take some time to look up Scripture passages that remind and encourage you to persevere toward your eternal goal, even in times of tumult and loss.

Where might you display your favorite passage in order to keep God's Word in the forefront of your mind? Would you like to hang it on your wall? Attach it to your refrigerator? Lay it on your nightstand? Use it as a bookmark? Or keep it in the best place possible, memorize it?

"There are two goals, vice and virtue, and both require perseverance. If you would reach life, you must persevere in virtue, and if you would reach eternal death, persevere in vice."

—St. Catherine of Siena

Journaling Space

"Therefore, since we are surrounded by so great a cloud of witnesses, let us rid ourselves of every burden and sin that clings to us and persevere in running the race that lies before us while keeping our eyes fixed on Jesus, the leader and perfecter of faith. For the sake of the joy that lay before him he endured the cross, despising its shame, and has taken his seat at the right of the throne of God. Consider how he endured such opposition from sinners, in order that you may not grow weary and lose heart."

—*Hebrews 12:1-3*

10th Star: Acceptance

Remember that you are in the holy presence of God. Close your eyes and take a deep breath. Ask God to reveal to you what you spend time rejecting in your thoughts, over and over again.

Spiritual Exercise

You were placed on this Earth in this time and place for a reason. God did not blindly lead you to where you are now; and if you have taken a wrong turn and deviated from the path He chose, He will show you how to turn back. Nothing He has led you to, or through, has been done without divine purpose. The Lord has a plan for you.

Only through acceptance of what you cannot change in your particular circumstances, in others, and in yourself, will you be able to turn "evil into good." Is there a situation at hand that you tend to reject in your spirit? Is there someone, something, or a situation that you have a difficult time accepting and spend energy fighting against? If you were to turn this difficulty or irritation over to the Lord and accept it as His gift to you, how might this change your outlook and relationship with Him?

"If God gives you an abundant harvest of trials,
it is a sign of great holiness which he desires you to attain.
Do you want to become a great saint?
Ask God to send you many sufferings."

—St. Ignatius of Loyola

Journaling Space

"See that no one returns evil for evil; rather, always seek what is good [both] for each other and for all. Rejoice always. Pray without ceasing. In all circumstances give thanks, for this is the will of God for you in Christ Jesus."
——*1 Thessalonians 5:15-18*

11th Star: Patience

Remember that you are in the holy presence of God. Close your eyes and take a deep breath. Ask God to remind you of the many and varied ways He has been patient with you throughout your life.

Spiritual Exercise

God is exceedingly patient with us, in our insecurities, our mistakes, our disobedience; and He calls us to treat others in kind. But when we don't get our way, impatience can incite anger and irritation toward ourselves, others, and God.

Reflect on a time when someone showed you great patience. How did experiencing this virtue in them make you feel? Contrarily, recall a time when someone showed impatience with you, and reflect upon how that made you feel.

How has impatience affected you and your relationships? Has it drawn you away from intimacy with Christ Jesus? The next time impatience provokes you, pause, slow down, take a deep breath, utter a prayer, and then respond—or perhaps, do nothing at all.

*"Let nothing perturb you, nothing frighten you. All things pass.
God does not change. Patience achieves everything."*

—St. Teresa of Avila

Journaling Space

"See that no one returns evil for evil; rather, always seek what is good [both] for each other and for all. Rejoice always. Pray without ceasing. In all circumstances give thanks, for this is the will of God for you in Christ Jesus. "We urge you, brothers, admonish the idle, cheer the fainthearted, support the weak, be patient with all."
—*1 Thessalonians 5:14*

12th Star: Humility

Remember that you are in the holy presence of God. Close your eyes and take a deep breath. Ask Mary to assist you in daily life to make yourself smaller, so that the Lord may shine brighter through you.

Spiritual Exercise

Pride comes to us in the most subtle of disguises: hoping for recognition, thinking ourselves better than another, disassociating from the unpopular or unattractive. . . In what circumstances does pride most easily take hold of you?

As painful and humiliating as it may feel, practice humbling yourself before God today and in the days to come when He prompts you to. And if your ego is wounded, allow your pride to melt in the crucible of silence. What kind of masterpiece might God make of you, if in humility, you allow Him full room to work?

"Do you wish to rise? Begin by descending.
You plan a tower that will pierce the clouds?
Lay first the foundation of humility."

—St. Augustine

Journaling Space

"So humble yourselves under the mighty hand of God,
that he may exalt you in due time."
—1 Peter 5:6

13th Star: Knowledge

Remember that you are in the holy presence of God. Close your eyes and take a deep breath. Ask the Holy Spirit for the gift of knowledge so that you might use it to bring great glory to God.

Spiritual Exercise

The Holy Spirit wishes to bestow upon us His gift of knowledge to the degree that we are able to receive it. However, we must cultivate this gift by continuing to study our faith. Do we take the time to read Sacred Scripture? Have we opened and examined the Catechism of the Catholic Church? Do we stop to listen each day, giving the Lord our silent and full attention?

In what ways are you doing your part to better know Jesus Christ and His ways? Decide upon an action you can reasonably commit to each week that would better inform you of your faith. Seek to know the Lord today so He can guide you tomorrow.

"Ignorance of Scripture is ignorance of Christ."

—St. Jerome

Journaling Space

"Whatever gains I had, these I have come to consider a loss because of Christ. More than that, I even consider everything as a loss because of the supreme good of knowing Christ Jesus my Lord. For his sake I have accepted the loss of all things and I consider them so much rubbish, that I may gain Christ and be found in him."

—*Philippians 3:7-9*

14th Star: Meekness

Remember that you are in the holy presence of God. Close your eyes and take a deep breath.
Pray to the Father for the grace to see meekness as a strength within yourself.

Spiritual Exercise

Our ego can provide us with a facade of power, strength, and self-assurance. In reality, however, it is a temporary edifice built on shifting sands, which breeds stress, negative emotions, fear, and insecurity. For when the ego's worldly props are taken away, on what will it stand?

In what areas do you notice your ego's insatiable demands? Does it insist on being right? Looking good? Forcing God's hand? Receiving love from those who cannot give it? Being in control? Feeling pleasure? Enjoying success? In what ways does your ego cause you unnecessary stress?

"Jesus gave me to know the depth of His meekness and humility and to understand that He clearly demanded the same of me. I felt the gaze of God in my soul. This filled me with unspeakable love, but I understand that the Lord was looking with love on my virtues and my heroic efforts, and I knew that this was what was drawing God into my heart. It is from this that I have come to understand that it is not enough for me to strive only for the ordinary virtues, but that I must try to exercise the heroic virtues. Although exteriorly a thing may be quite ordinary, it is the different manner [in which it is carried out] that only the eye of God catches."

—St. Faustina Kowalska

Journaling Space

"Blessed are the meek, for they will inherit the land."
—*Matthew* 5:5

15th Star: Fortitude

Remember that you are in the holy presence of God. Close your eyes and take a deep breath. Ask that any fear in your heart be replaced with courage.

Spiritual Exercise

Can you recall a time in your life when you feared the worst, and yet somehow you exhibited fortitude, bravely handling the task or situation at hand? You are the Father's child. As a good, earthly father both nurtures His children and challenges them to grow in courage, so your Father in heaven does the same for you. When your knees are weak, He will uphold you. In His abounding love and care, He will infuse your soul with strength. But you must ask this of Him, put your complete trust in Him, and refuse to care about the opinions of the world. Others, and even you, will marvel at your courage when they see the power of the Father in you.

The next time that fear grips you, how might you allow your Father to soothe your nerves, steady your voice, and allay any anxious thoughts?

"We fear the future because we are wasting today."

—St. Mother Teresa

Journaling Space

"O Most High, when I am afraid,
in you I place my trust.
I praise the word of God;
I trust in God, I do not fear.
What can mere flesh do to me?
——*Psalm* 56:3-5

16th Star: Constancy

Remember that you are in the holy presence of God. Close your eyes and take a deep breath. Ask God to remove or help you to resist the distractions in your life that dampen your spiritual growth.

Spiritual Exercise

God is so delighted, consoled, and grateful to you for sharing your heart and time with Him. Almost nothing could please Him more. Make a list of creative ways you would like to pray. Are you ready to commit to doing one, two—all of them?

Now make another list of the things that distract you from prayer and from God, things you know you'd be better off not doing. Then ask yourself, "Am I ready to let them go?"

"Never give up prayer, and should you find dryness and difficulty, persevere in it for this very reason. God often desires to see what love your soul has, and love is not tried by ease and satisfaction."

—*St. John of the Cross*

Journaling Space

"Let your eyes look straight ahead
and your gaze be focused forward.
Survey the path for your feet,
and all your ways will be sure.
Turn neither to right nor to left,
keep your foot far from evil."
—*Proverbs 4:25-27*

17th Star: Goodness

Remember that you are in the holy presence of God. Close your eyes and take a deep breath.
Pray for the grace to see the goodness within yourself.

Spiritual Exercise

Jesus—Who is holy, perfect, and all-consuming love—lives within you. In response to betrayal, mockery, disdain, and persecution, He offered goodness in return. How might you adopt the same response to the evil in your life? In what circumstances is it difficult for you to be good?

Is there an area of your personality where goodness comes easily, and others have noticed it in you? Do you see the goodness in yourself?

"Yours is the gigantic task of overcoming all evil with good, always trying amidst the problems of life to place your trust in God, knowing that his grace supplies strength to human weakness. You must oppose every form of hatred with the invincible power of Christ's love."

—St. Pope John Paul II

Journaling Space

"You have heard that it was said, 'You shall love your neighbor and hate your enemy.' But I say to you, love your enemies, and pray for those who persecute you, that you may be children of your heavenly Father, for he makes his sun rise on the bad and the good, and causes rain to fall on the just and the unjust. For if you love those who love you, what recompense will you have? Do not the tax collectors do the same? And if you greet your brothers only, what is unusual about that? Do not the pagans do the same? So be perfect, just as your heavenly Father is perfect."

—— *Matthew 5:43-48*

18th Star: Self-Control

Remember that you are in the holy presence of God. Close your eyes and take a deep breath.
Ask for Mary's intercession for the gift of self-control, even in moments when you feel you have none.

Spiritual Exercise

Christ Jesus and His Holy Mother endured unthinkable hardships throughout the Lord's Passion. Imagine what horrible feelings could have overtaken and undone them both. Their agony was indescribable, and yet their every action was in line with God's Will, in harmony with love.

Reflect upon times past when you have felt out of control. In what situations can you feel undone? Are there recurring themes in your life that overwhelm you with uncomfortable feelings?

Remind yourself to call upon God's indwelling Spirit of self-control.

"If anyone strives to be delivered from his troubles out of love of God, he will strive patiently, gently, humbly, and calmly, looking for deliverance rather to God's goodness and providence than to his own industry or efforts; but if self-love is the prevailing object he will grow hot and eager in seeking relief, as though all depended more upon himself than upon God. . . This unresting anxiety is the greatest evil which can happen to the soul, sin only excepted."

—St. Francis de Sales

Journaling Space

"For God did not give us a spirit of cowardice but rather of power and love and self-control."
—2 Timothy 1:7

19th Star: Attentiveness

Remember that you are in the holy presence of God. Close your eyes and take a deep breath. Ask for the grace to see those around you, each day, as God sees them.

Spiritual Exercise

You have lonely neighbors, suffering neighbors, hungry neighbors. Do you notice them? Do you see Jesus in their eyes? Or are they mere fleeting shadows? In God's will, there are no mistakes. It is not by happenstance that you encounter and interact with the people you do. God has a plan and a purpose for their presence in your life, and if you are attentive to the Holy Spirit, then you will see your neighbor. How would you measure your attentiveness toward the people around you?

*"Being unwanted, unloved, uncared for, forgotten by everybody,
I think that is a much greater hunger, a much greater poverty
than the person who has nothing to eat."*
—St. Mother Teresa

Journaling Space

"You shall love the Lord your God with all your heart, with all your soul, with all your mind, and with all your strength.' The second is this: 'You shall love your neighbor as yourself.' There is no other commandment greater than these."
——*Mark 12:30-31*

20th Star: Faith

Remember that you are in the holy presence of God. Close your eyes and take a deep breath. Ask Mary to help you to see through the appearances of the world into the depths of faith.

Spiritual Exercise

Mother Mary, Spiritual Vessel of Our Savior, said yes to carrying Jesus in her womb. In her humanity, she lacked understanding, yet through her faith, God could still within her any wavering confusion or fear.

Ask Mary to reveal to you, now, the size of your faith. Is it so small as to be invisible? Is it the size of a mustard seed? A tree? A mountain?

The world will inevitably disappoint you, but God never will. Mary had no doubts of the unending goodness and trustworthiness of her Lord. Ask the Blessed Mother, the only person, aside from Jesus, to have possessed the fullness of all virtue, to pray for an increase in your faith.

"Do not abandon yourselves to despair.
We are the Easter people and Hallelujah is our song."

—St. Pope John Paul II

Journaling Space

"... Whoever is begotten by God conquers the world. And the victory that conquers the world is our faith."

—*1 John 5:4*

21st Star: Counsel

Remember that you are in the holy presence of God. Close your eyes and take a deep breath. Ask the Holy Spirit for His gift of counsel. Ask Him to reveal something He wishes for you to do.

Spiritual Exercise

In those times when the Holy Spirit enlightens your mind to understand the people and situations around you, to see right from wrong, and to know the right path—are you of a temperament that tends to be either too quick or too shy to speak words of counsel? When you do speak, are your words more inclined to be too harsh or not strong enough?

"But while extremely sensitive as to the slightest approach to slander, you must also guard against an extreme into which some people fall, who, in their desire to speak evil of no one, actually uphold and speak well of vice."

—St. Frances de Sales

Journaling Space

"My brothers, if anyone among you should stray from the truth and someone bring him back, he should know that whoever brings back a sinner from the error of his way will save his soul from death and will cover a multitude of sins."

—*James 5:19-20*

22nd Star: Renunciation

Remember that you are in the holy presence of God. Close your eyes and take a deep breath. Ask Mary to gently reveal to you an area of sin in your life that you haven't wanted to see.

Spiritual Exercise

The people closest to us sometimes point out our defects, which can sting us with emotional force. This can offend us to the degree that we retreat into denial or respond by pointing out their defects. Yet our accusers are sometimes right—if not in tone, then in truth.

What sin has someone pointed out in you? If you denied it and later realized that they were right, or if you allowed their comment to crush you with self-condemnation, promise yourself that you will take this sin to the Sacrament of Reconciliation to be free from it.

"Thus it sometimes happens that temptation in itself is sin to us, because we have ourselves brought it upon us. For instance, if I know that gaming leads me to passion and blasphemy, and that all play is temptation to me, I sin each and every time that I play, and I am responsible for all the temptations which may come upon me at the gaming table. So again, if I know that certain society involves me in temptation to evil, and yet I voluntarily seek it, I am unquestionably responsible for all that I may encounter in the way of temptation therein."

—St. Frances de Sales

Journaling Space

"Now the works of the flesh are obvious: immorality, impurity, licentiousness, idolatry, sorcery, hatreds, rivalry, jealousy, outbursts of fury, acts of selfishness, dissensions, factions, occasions of envy, drinking bouts, orgies, and the like. I warn you, as I warned you before, that those who do such things will not inherit the kingdom of God. In contrast, the fruit of the Spirit is love, joy, peace, patience, kindness, generosity, faithfulness, gentleness, self-control. Against such there is no law. Now those who belong to Christ [Jesus] have crucified their flesh with its passions and desires. If we live in the Spirit, let us also follow the Spirit."
——*Galatians 5:19-25*

23rd Star: Surrender

Remember that you are in the holy presence of God. Close your eyes and take a deep breath. Ask Jesus to show you an area of your life that He would like you to surrender to Him, rather than have you try to control.

Spiritual Exercise

Life is stressful, and we often make it more stressful than necessary. How tightly do you hold on to your will? Our anxious pursuit of what we want, and our strenuous avoidance of what we don't, can bring even more agitation to our spirits, not mention illness to our bodies. Our dissatisfaction over the way others are, or the way we ourselves are, can compound our misery.

How might the acceptance of yourself as God made you, and your resignation to the things you cannot change, allow you to more fully surrender to Christ? How might your reliance on God to fix what you can't fix, and to do what you can't do, bring you closer to Him and to inward peace and joy? What do you think life would be like if you fully surrendered your will to the Lord of your life?

"Take, Lord, and receive all my liberty, my memory, my understanding, and my entire will, all I have and call my own. You have given all to me. To you, Lord, I return it. Everything is yours; do with it what you will. Give me only your love and your grace, that is enough for me."

—St. Ignatius of Loyola

Journaling Space

"Woe to anyone who contends with their Maker; a potsherd among potsherds of the earth! Shall the clay say to the potter, 'What are you doing?' or, 'What you are making has no handles?'"

—*Isaiah 45:9*

24th Star: Friendliness

Remember that you are in the holy presence of God. Close your eyes and take a deep breath.
Ask Jesus to fill you with His joy.

Spiritual Exercise

Sometimes it helps to ask someone close to us (someone who loves us and is honest) how they see us. "Am I friendly?" you might ask them. "Do you see me as someone who exudes joy?" Their answer could provide insight into how you are seen and how your presence influences the world around you.

How would you like to be perceived? How would you like to affect the people around you?

*"Do good everywhere, so that everyone can say:
'This is a son of Christ.'"*

—St. Padre Pio

Journaling Space

"Let love be sincere; hate what is evil, hold on to what is good; love one another with mutual affection; anticipate one another in showing honor. Do not grow slack in zeal, be fervent in spirit, serve the Lord. Rejoice in hope, endure in affliction, persevere in prayer. Contribute to the needs of the holy ones, exercise hospitality. Bless those who persecute [you], bless and do not curse them. Rejoice with those who rejoice, weep with those who weep. Have the same regard for one another; do not be haughty but associate with the lowly; do not be wise in your own estimation. Do not repay anyone evil for evil; be concerned for what is noble in the sight of all. If possible, on your part, live at peace with all."

——*Romans 12:9-18*

25th Star: Diligence

Remember that you are in the holy presence of God. Close your eyes and take a deep breath. Take a moment to ask Jesus if He is pleased with how you are setting aside time every day to pray.

Spiritual Exercise

Have you noticed that you always have plenty of time for the things that you love, but there is never enough time for the things that you don't? Some people dread, avoid, or find little joy in prayer because they spend that time worriedly digging into their troubles, rather than focusing on the Lord.

It is so much harder to be diligent in prayer, if prayer is more a matter of discipline than desire. Turn your thoughts heavenward. Look up to Jesus who walked on water. Keep from peering down into the stormy seas. The more you gaze at Him, the more prayer will be a joy.

"Whether, therefore, we receive what we ask for, or do not receive it, let us still continue steadfast in prayer. For to fail in obtaining the desires of our heart, when God so wills it, is not worse than to receive it; for we know not as He does, what is profitable to us."

—St. John Chrysostom

Journaling Space

"This saying is trustworthy: If we have died with him we shall also live with him; if we persevere we shall also reign with him. But if we deny him he will deny us. If we are unfaithful he remains faithful, for he cannot deny himself."

—2 Timothy 2:11-14

26th Star: Respect

Remember that you are in the holy presence of God. Close your eyes and take a deep breath. Ask the Lord to remove any condescension, judgment, or disrespect you have toward anyone.

Spiritual Exercise

When we are treated disrespectfully, as if our lives and our feelings do not matter, it can feel like we've been offered a dose of spiritual and emotional poison. If we respond in the same manner, then that poison is swallowed; we lose the spiritual battle, and our souls become tarnished with sin and sadness. How difficult is it for you to show respect to those who do not respect you—or to those you feel do not deserve respect?

"Always think of yourself as everyone's servant; look for Christ Our Lord in everyone and you will then have respect and reverence for them all."

—St. Teresa of Avila

Journaling Space

"With the fruit of one's mouth one's belly is filled,
with the produce of one's lips one is sated.
Death and life are in the power of the tongue;
those who choose one shall eat its fruit."
——*Proverbs 18:20-21*

27th Star: Hope

Remember that you are in the holy presence of God. Close your eyes and take a deep breath. Ask the Trinity to pour hope into your soul and remove any doubt or despair.

Spiritual Exercise

Where do you place your hope? In the things and people and dreams of this world? Or in God? This is often a choice that we are not consciously aware of. Not much can be accomplished in the spiritual life without the supernatural virtue of hope. Hope is enough to carry us through valleys of extreme hardship and deprivation. Hope can see what the naked eye cannot and passes easily into new worlds of possibilities.

Are there promises that God has made to you, through Scripture and His Church, that help renew your spirit? How has the Lord reached out to you to remind you of the hope that you do have in Him?

"God wishes us not to rest upon anything but His infinite goodness; do not let us expect anything, hope anything, or desire anything but from Him, and let us put our trust and confidence in Him alone."

—St. Charles Borromeo

Journaling Space

"For I know well the plans I have in mind for you, plans for your welfare and not for woe, so as to give you a future of hope."
—*Jeremiah 29:11*

28th Star: Resiliency

Remember that you are in the holy presence of God. Close your eyes and take a deep breath. Give thanks to God the Father for His unwavering support and outstretched hand.

Spiritual Exercise

You are a Child of the Father, and not of just any Father, but the Almighty Creator of heaven and Earth, time and eternity. Your Father—Who parted the Red Sea for safe passage, Who raised His Son Jesus on the third day, Who brings light from pure darkness and peace from raging turmoil—will not abandon you. When life feels unmanageable and burdensome, what will remind you to reach out and grasp His hand so that He can give you a resilient spirit, no matter life's circumstances?

"Pray, hope, and don't worry."

—St. Padre Pio

Journaling Space

"For though the fig tree does not blossom, and no fruit appears on the vine,
Though the yield of the olive fails and the terraces produce no nourishment,
Though the flocks disappear from the fold and there is no herd in the stalls,
Yet I will rejoice in the LORD and exult in my saving God.
GOD, my Lord, is my strength; he makes my feet swift as those of deer
and enables me to tread upon the heights."
—— *Habakkuk 3:17-19*

29th Star: Detachment

Remember that you are in the holy presence of God. Close your eyes and take a deep breath. Confide in the Lord: "Jesus, I trust in you. Deliver me from my bondage to the things of this world."

Spiritual Exercise

The grief that comes with loss and change is necessary in life, yet never welcome. Practicing spiritual detachment is not easy, especially when we undergo the agony of losing a loved one, or the stripping away of possessions, a home, or our good reputation. Yet the more we are free from disordered affections, the more gracefully we will pass through the painful questioning and the depressive feelings that come with any earthly loss. The only way possible to acquire lasting peace and joy is to cling more tightly to the Lord and relax our emotional reliance on the things of this world. Ask God now to help you transfer one of your temporal attachments onto the One Who created all and in Whom nothing good and lovely is ever lost.

"In order to be united with Him, the will must consequently be emptied of and detached from all disordered appetite and satisfaction with respect to every particular thing in which it can rejoice, whether earthly or heavenly, temporal or spiritual, so that purged and cleansed of all inordinate satisfactions, joys, and appetites it might be wholly occupied in loving God with its affections."

—St. John of the Cross

Journaling Space

"I tell you, brothers, the time is running out. From now on, let those having wives act as not having them, those weeping as not weeping, those rejoicing as not rejoicing, those buying as not owning, those using the world as not using it fully. For the world in its present form is passing away."

——*1 Corinthians 7:29-31*

30th Star: Poverty

Remember that you are in the holy presence of God. Close your eyes and take a deep breath.
Ask Jesus to help you to live simply and love the poor, as He did.

Spiritual Exercise

The Gospel commands us to serve the poor and warns us not to store up wealth for ourselves. But do we aid the materially and spiritually less fortunate? Do we, as St. Mother Teresa said, "Live simply so that others may simply live"? Or is our lifestyle so far removed from the poor that we easily forget they exist?

There are people around us with hardened exteriors whose hearts weep daily. They can be unpleasant. The person on the sidewalk with the cardboard sign may be an uncomfortable sight, while the angry atheist in the office may be disagreeable to speak with. Are there people or areas you avoid so that the burden of them does not come near you? How would Jesus have you respond to them?

"I choose the poverty of our poor people.
But I am grateful to receive it [the Nobel Peace Prize] in the name of the hungry,
the naked, the homeless, of the crippled, of the blind, of the lepers, of all those people
who feel unwanted, unloved, uncared for throughout society, people that have become
a burden to the society and are shunned by everyone."

—St. Mother Teresa

Journaling Space

"When Jesus heard this he said to him, 'There is still one thing left for you: sell all that you have and distribute it to the poor, and you will have a treasure in heaven. Then come, follow me.' But when he heard this he became quite sad, for he was very rich. Jesus looked at him and said, 'How hard it is for those who have wealth to enter the kingdom of God! For it is easier for a camel to pass through the eye of a needle than for a rich person to enter the kingdom of God.'"

——*Luke 28:22-30*

31st Star: Wisdom

Remember that you are in the holy presence of God. Close your eyes and take a deep breath.
Think of a problem you are dealing with. Pray and ask for guidance.
"What is the next step from here, Lord?"

Spiritual Exercise

Jesus gave sight to a blind man, and He wishes to give insight and vision to you. Wisdom is cultivated by means of your relationship with God. The more intimate your union with Him, the more He will reveal to you new knowledge that is forever old, and vast landscapes that have been hidden in plain sight. King Solomon prayed for wisdom above all else and received "her." Have you also asked for this gift?

"What more do you want, O soul! And what else do you search for outside, when within yourself you possess your riches, delights, satisfactions, fullness, and kingdom—your Beloved Whom you desire and seek? Be joyful and gladdened in your interior recollection with Him, for you have Him so close to you. Desire Him there, adore Him there. Do not go in pursuit of Him outside yourself. You will only become distracted and wearied thereby, and you shall not find Him, nor enjoy Him more securely, nor sooner, nor more intimately than by seeking Him within you."

—St. John of the Cross

Journaling Space

"Therefore I prayed, and prudence was given me; I pleaded and the spirit of Wisdom came to me. I preferred her to scepter and throne, and deemed riches nothing in comparison with her, nor did I liken any priceless gem to her; because all gold, in view of her, is a bit of sand, and before her, silver is to be accounted mire. Beyond health and beauty I loved her, and I chose to have her rather than the light, because her radiance never ceases. Yet all good things together came to me with her, and countless riches at her hands; I rejoiced in them all, because Wisdom is their leader, though I had not known that she is their mother."

—— Wisdom 7:7-12

32nd Star: Discipline

Remember that you are in the holy presence of God. Close your eyes and take a deep breath.
Ask Mary to teach you how to love that which is good for you.

Spiritual Exercise

When you practice the virtue of discipline, harnessing your mental and physical faculties to accomplish your goals, do you make sure that those goals are ones God has asked of you? Discipline is not a virtue when applied to selfish endeavors, which are time and effort wasted in the eyes of heaven. To what tasks do you apply yourself in a disciplined manner?

An often neglected, but profoundly important discipline for the soul is spiritual reading. As St. Vincent de Paul once commented, "Read some chapter of a devout book. . . It is very easy and most necessary, for just as you speak to God when at prayer, God speaks to you when you read." St. Padre Pio also said, "The harm that comes to souls from the lack of reading holy books makes me shudder. . . What power spiritual reading has to lead to a change of course, and to make even worldly people enter into the way of perfection."

*"Everyone knows that not to go forward on this road is to turn back,
and not to gain ground is to lose."*

—St. John of the Cross

Journaling Space

"If you will give these instructions to the brothers, you will be a good minister of Christ Jesus, nourished on the words of the faith and of the sound teaching you have followed. Avoid profane and silly myths. Train yourself for devotion, for, while physical training is of limited value, devotion is valuable in every respect, since it holds a promise of life both for the present and for the future. This saying is trustworthy and deserves full acceptance. For this we toil and struggle, because we have set our hope on the living God, who is the savior of all, especially of those who believe."

——1 Timothy 4:6-10

33rd Star: Mortification

Spiritual Exercise

Scripture teaches us that some demons can only be cast out by prayer and fasting (some versions of Mark 9:29). Interior and exterior mortifications—small and large sacrifices offered with great love—are weapons of spiritual warfare. They purify our souls and can effect healings, conversions, and miracles.

Pick one of your habits or senses that if left unchecked causes you and others harm. Today, make at act of mortification and deny yourself the temporary satisfaction it offers.

"Endeavor to be inclined always: not to the easiest, but to the most difficult; not to the most delightful, but to the most distasteful; not to the most gratifying, but to the less pleasant; not to what means rest for you, but to hard work; not to the consoling, but to the unconsoling; not to the most, but to the least; not to the highest and most precious, but to the lowest and most despised; not to wanting something, but to wanting nothing. Do not go about looking for the best of temporal things, but for the worst, and, for Christ, desire to enter into complete nakedness, emptiness, and poverty in everything in the world."

—St. John of the Cross

Journaling Space

"Enter through the narrow gate; for the gate is wide and the road broad that leads to destruction, and those who enter through it are many. How narrow the gate and constricted the road that leads to life. And those who find it are few."

——*Matthew 7:13-14*

34th Star: Boldness

Remember that you are in the holy presence of God. Close your eyes and take a deep breath. Pray for the Holy Spirit to fill your soul with the same boldness that He gave to the apostles.

Spiritual Exercise

In moments when we are called to holy boldness, there is a stirring in the deep recesses of our souls that calls us into unknown, sometimes scary territory. When this happens to you, the Holy is preparing to use your voice, your body, your presence to further the Kingdom and proclaim the Gospel. Do you trust Him to steady your hands, direct your feet, and shape your words? How does it feel when you refuse to respond to such promptings out of fear? How does it feel when you take a step forward in holy boldness?

Make a point to break out of your comfort zone today and push through a fear that has been holding you back. Certain fears leave us only when we walk boldly through them. They may look like strong, towering walls, but upon impact, they crumble and turn to dust.

"The proud man who trusts in himself may well undertake nothing, but the humble man is all the braver that he knows his own helplessness, and his courage waxes in proportion to his low opinion of himself, because all his trust is in God, Who delights to show forth His Power in our weakness, His Mercy in our misery."

—St. Frances de Sales

Journaling Space

"So they called them back and ordered them not to speak or teach at all in the name of Jesus. Peter and John, however, said to them in reply, "Whether it is right in the sight of God for us to obey you rather than God, you be the judges. It is impossible for us not to speak about what we have seen and heard."

—*Acts 4:18-20*

35th Star: Understanding

Remember that you are in the holy presence of God. Close your eyes and take a deep breath. Take a moment to thank God the Father for creating you so intricately and beautifully in His image.

Spiritual Exercise

Though created in God's image, we need only to look up at the sky and contemplate the universe, or imagine Jesus saying from the Cross, "Father, forgive them, they know not what they do," to realize how small our understanding of God must be. Only through the pursuit of true understanding and the willingness to accept Jesus as God come to Earth, do we begin to comprehend His essence, His love, and His teachings.

Is there a teaching on faith and morals that Jesus Christ has passed on to us through Scripture and His Church that you disagree with or simply cannot grasp? Ask Mary to pray for you for the gift of understanding. She will always help you. Jesus would not give us His Church with His teachings only to later tell us some were right and some were wrong, all along. He never told us to figure it out ourselves, individually, on our own. Instead, he said, "And so I say to you, you are Peter, and upon this rock I will build my church, and the gates of the netherworld shall not prevail against it" (Matthew 16:18).

"God judged it better to bring good out of evil than to suffer no evil to exist."

—St. Augustine

Journaling Space

"He said to them, "But who do you say that I am?" Simon Peter said in reply, "You are the Messiah, the Son of the living God." Jesus said to him in reply, "Blessed are you, Simon son of Jonah. For flesh and blood has not revealed this to you, but my heavenly Father. And so I say to you, you are Peter, and upon this rock I will build my church, and the gates of the netherworld shall not prevail against it."

—— *Matthew 16:15-18*

36th Star: Prudence

Remember that you are in the holy presence of God. Close your eyes and take a deep breath. Ask Our Lady to come by your side and help you take your next steps with prudence.

Spiritual Exercise

Prudence can be hard won. It is often the reward of many mistakes and scars that remind us of what not to do, because we have done it before—to our failure and dismay. Prudence requires hindsight, foresight, and present-sight, and it petitions God for all three. Imprudence refuses to contemplate or accept the weight and consequences of our thoughts and actions, and it therefore lunges us blindly into the future.

Our Lady never shouldered any undertaking or spoke serious words without first aligning herself in prayer with the Lord's will. As you go through your day, remind yourself to consult God before you speak or act, asking Him what He would have you do or say. Make this a lifelong habit and the virtue of prudence will direct your steps, paving a trail of no regret.

"Virtue without prudence is not virtue at all. We should often pray to the Holy Spirit for this grace of prudence. Prudence consists in discretion, rational reflection and courageous resolution. The final decision is always up to us."

—St. Faustina Kowalska

Journaling Space

"Does not Wisdom call, and Understanding raise her voice? On the top of the heights along the road, at the crossroads she takes her stand; By the gates at the approaches of the city, in the entryways she cries aloud: "To you, O people, I call; my appeal is to you mortals. You naive ones, gain prudence, you fools, gain sense."

—*Proverbs 8:1-5*

37th Star: Piety

Remember that you are in the holy presence of God. Close your eyes and take a deep breath. Ask the saints, our models in piety, to help mold and shape you into one of them.

Spiritual Exercise

The gift of piety enables us to see in God not only our sovereign Master, but a loving Dad to Whom we can cry out with trust and intimacy, "Abba, Father!" (Romans 8:15). Imbued with the gift of piety, we see our religion not as a set of rules and obligations, but as our Father's blueprint of love. Only when we fall in love do His requirements of love make sense. Our soul is moved with an affectionate obedience that wants to do what He commands because we love the One who commands.

What would you say to God if He were to ask you right now, "Do you love Me?"

"*Late have I loved you, Beauty so old and so new, late have I loved you! For you were within me and I was outside, and there searched for you, and in my unloveliness, I rushed to the lovely things you made. You were with me, and I was not with you. They kept me far from you, those things which would not be if they were not in you. You called and cried out and burst my deafness; you sparked, and shone and banished my blindness; you were fragrant and my breath was drawn, and I inhaled you; I tasted you and crave you and thirst for you; you touched me, and I have burned for your peace.*"

—St. Augustine

Journaling Space

"I will give you a new heart, and a new spirit I will put within you. I will remove the heart of stone from your flesh and give you a heart of flesh. I will put my spirit within you so that you walk in my statutes, observe my ordinances, and keep them. You will live in the land I gave to your ancestors; you will be my people, and I will be your God."

—*Ezekiel 36:26-28*

38th Star: Justice

Remember that you are in the holy presence of God. Close your eyes and take a deep breath. Ask God for an open heart to hear the cries of the unjustly afflicted.

Spiritual Exercise

God is the advocate for the defenseless, the freer of the slave, the admonisher of the proud, and the voice of the persecuted. He is the Just Judge and the last Word. In the end, no one "gets away" with anything. Those who perpetrate injustice and remain unrepentant will be punished, and those who fight for justice will be rewarded. In what ways are you being called to speak and act on behalf of God's justice?

In order to effectively fight for justice in the world, we are called to be just in our own lives. Scripture says that St. Joseph was a just man (Matthew 1:10). Mary exalted God's justice in her Magnificat. Would God say that you are a just man or woman?

"We ought to speak, shout out against injustices,
with confidence and without fear. We proclaim the principles of the Church, the reign of love,
without forgetting that it is also a reign of justice."

— Blessed Miguel Pro

Journaling Space

"And Mary said: 'My soul proclaims the greatness of the Lord; my spirit rejoices in God my savior. For he has looked upon his handmaid's lowliness; behold, from now on will all ages call me blessed. The Mighty One has done great things for me, and holy is his name. His mercy is from age to age to those who fear him. He has shown might with his arm, dispersed the arrogant of mind and heart. He has thrown down the rulers from their thrones but lifted up the lowly. The hungry he has filled with good things; the rich he has sent away empty. He has helped Israel his servant, remembering his mercy, according to his promise to our fathers, to Abraham and to his descendants forever.'"

—*Luke 1:46-55*

39th Star: Peace

Remember that you are in the holy presence of God. Close your eyes and take a deep breath. Thank Jesus for coming as the Prince of Peace.

Spiritual Exercise

Worry is the thief of peace. Ascending the mountain of holiness by striving for virtue in alignment with God's will is the only guaranteed way of attaining a life of inner peace. How might your perspective change if you allowed God to wipe away your worry? What could you accomplish without the burden of fear?

Is there a worry you would like God to remove now? Imagine yourself releasing it into His hands with complete trust—and your soul being filled with peace.

*"For the soul is always afraid
until she has attained true love."*
—St. Catherine of Siena

Journaling Space

"Have no anxiety at all, but in everything, by prayer and petition, with thanksgiving, make your requests known to God. Then the peace of God that surpasses all understanding will guard your hearts and minds in Christ Jesus."
—*Philippians 4:6-7*

40th Star: Excellence

Spiritual Exercise

Do you pursue excellence in your job, hobby, ministry, family, relationships, spiritual life, or something else? Have you ever accomplished something to the point of excellence? Did you do so for the glory of God and His Kingdom, or for a different goal? What were the fruits of that achievement?

How might you see your planning, actions, and outcomes changing if the ultimate goal in your pursuit of excellence is the promulgation of the Gospel?

"Pray as though everything depended on God. Work as though everything depended on you."

—*St. Augustine*

Journaling Space

"Therefore, my beloved brothers, be firm, steadfast, always fully devoted to the work of the Lord, knowing that in the Lord your labor is not in vain."
——*1 Corinthians 15:58*

41st Star: Temperance

Remember that you are in the holy presence of God. Close your eyes and take a deep breath. Thank God for His gift of free will, and ask Him to help you conform your will to His.

Spiritual Exercise

Temperance is an act of exercising control and moderation over our physical and emotional appetites. We exchange limited, temporary satisfaction for lasting peace. In what ways do your desires override your self-restraint? Do you suffer from an addiction that throws temperance to the wind? How might you reach out for and receive help with an addiction or a habit of overindulgence? Do you believe God's grace is sufficient for you to triumph over your weakness? (2 Corinthians 12:9)

"If sensual affection wants to love sensual things, the eye of understanding is moved in that direction. It takes for its object only passing things with selfish love, contempt for virtue, and love of vice, drawing from these pride and impatience. And the memory is filled only with what affection holds out to it. This love so dazzles the eye that it neither discerns nor sees anything but the glitter of these things. Such is their glitter that understanding sees and affection loves them all as if their brightness came from goodness and loveliness. Were it not for this glitter, people would never sin, for the soul by her very nature cannot desire anything but good. But vice is disguised as something good for her, and so the soul sins. Her eyes, though, cannot tell the difference because of her blindness, and she does not know the truth. So she wanders about searching for what is good and lovely where it is not to be found."

—St. Catherine of Siena

Journaling Space

"If you find honey, eat only what you need,
lest you have your fill and vomit it up."
——*Proverbs 25:16*

42nd Star: Chastity

Remember that you are in the holy presence of God. Close your eyes and take a deep breath.
Ask Jesus for the gift to be chaste.

Spiritual Exercise

The virtue of chastity brings freedom of Spirit, the freedom to love others selflessly. Chastity in married life is self-giving love in physical intimacy between husband and wife. Chastity in the single life is more than just abstinence. It seeks to protect, honor, and respect others as equal creations made in the image of God and leaves the soul free to love. Contrarily, lust tries to possess, control, and devour the other, whom it reduces to an object. Lust cares nothing of the soul and seeks to drag us and the target of our desire toward damnation.

Jesus warns us sternly, "If your right eye causes you to sin, tear it out and throw it away. It is better for you to lose one of your members than to have your whole body thrown into Gehenna." (Matthew 5:29)

Take a moment to reflect on the way you view people to whom you are attracted. Do you look at them through the eyes of a pure heart? Do you stare at them through filters of sensuality and desire? Do you see lustful thoughts as temptations to sin, or as normal feelings that can safely be indulged?

"Until slumber comes to the appetites through the mortification of sensuality, and until this very sensuality is stilled in such a way that the appetites do not war against the spirit, the soul will not walk out to genuine freedom, to the enjoyment of union with its Beloved."

—St. John of the Cross

Journaling Space

"Do you not know that the unjust will not inherit the kingdom of God? Do not be deceived; neither fornicators nor idolaters nor adulterers nor boy prostitutes nor sodomites nor thieves nor the greedy nor drunkards nor slanderers nor robbers will inherit the kingdom of God. That is what some of you used to be; but now you have had yourselves washed, you were sanctified, you were justified in the name of the Lord Jesus Christ and in the Spirit of our God."
—*1 Corinthians 6:9-11*

43rd Star: Obedience

Remember that you are in the holy presence of God. Close your eyes and take a deep breath. Commit yourself to Jesus today: "Lord, I am Yours. What is it You wish for me to do?"

Spiritual Exercise

To follow Jesus and live out His teachings can be challenging. We live in a time when disobedience of God's commandments is celebrated, and steadfast obedience is mocked. Are there certain Church teachings or commandments you find especially difficult to follow? Have there been times in your life when your obedience to God was tested, but you passed safely through the storm? What helped you to succeed?

"It is not hard to obey when we love the one whom we obey."

—*St. Ignatius of Loyola*

Journaling Space

"Whoever has my commandments and observes them is the one who loves me. And whoever loves me will be loved by my Father, and I will love him and reveal myself to him."

—*John 14:21*

44th Star: Sacrifice

Remember that you are in the holy presence of God. Close your eyes and take a deep breath. Thank Jesus for His ultimate Sacrifice, without which there would be no eternal salvation.

Spiritual Exercise

The first thing Jesus commanded His apostles to do was to leave their old lives behind and follow Him. In the offering of this extreme and painful sacrifice, His followers emptied themselves of their worldly attachments, thereby opening themselves to receive and give great graces. In the same way, God uses your sacrifices to bring about miracles and breakthroughs in your life and the lives of others.

Is there something about which you repeatedly complain? Perhaps an item, action, situation, or person—even yourself? What sacrifices could you make to help bring about change?

"Bear the cross and do not make the cross bear you."

—St. Philip Neri

Journaling Space

"Then he said to all, 'If anyone wishes to come after me, he must deny himself and take up his cross daily and follow me. For whoever wishes to save his life will lose it, but whoever loses his life for my sake will save it. What profit is there for one to gain the whole world yet lose or forfeit himself?

—John 14:21

45th Star: Mercy

Remember that you are in the holy presence of God. Close your eyes and take a deep breath. Thank Jesus for His unfailing mercy and for bringing you into His light.

Spiritual Exercise

Have you ever offended someone or done something that deserved punishment? Did you get caught? If so, did you feel the sting of judgment or condemnation, or were you handled with mercy? How did it make you feel?

We will be judged in the same measure we judge others. We will receive mercy to the extent that we show mercy to others. A soul that cannot embrace its own need for mercy has none to offer. Do you believe you treat others mercifully? Why or why not?

"All grace flows from mercy, and the last hour abounds with mercy for us. Let no one doubt concerning the goodness of God; even if a person's sins were as dark as night, God's mercy is stronger than our misery. One thing alone is necessary, that the sinner set ajar the door of his heart, be it ever so little, to let in a ray of God's merciful Grace, and then God will do the rest."

—St. Faustina Kowalska

Journaling Space

"The **LORD**'s acts of mercy are not exhausted, his compassion is not spent;
They are renewed each morning—great is your faithfulness!"
— *Lamentations 3:22-23:22*

46th Star: Awe

Remember that you are in the holy presence of God. Close your eyes and take a deep breath. Imagine yourself standing before the Throne of God. What do you see? What do you feel?

Spiritual Exercise

What instills within you holy fear and awe of the Lord? A majestic landscape at sunset? A sentence that seems written just for you? The contagious laugh of an infant? The humility of a dying saint? Or is it the ominous sound of thunder? The consuming flames of a forest fire? The crumbling edifice of the Twin Towers?

Take the time to ponder the things that strike your heart with awe. Allow them to remind you that every instant of your life will be relived when you come before the Tribunal of the Lord. If you remember that you are standing in eternity right now, in the awesome presence of God, you will know how to live each moment of your life.

"When there is union of love, the image of the Beloved is so sketched in the will and drawn so vividly, that it is true to say that the Beloved lives in the lover and the lover in the Beloved. Love produces such likeness in this transformation of lovers that one can say each is the other and both are one. The reason is, that in the union and transformation of love, each gives possession of self to the other, and each leaves and exchanges self for the other. Thus each one lives in the other and is the other, and both are one in the transformation of love.

—St. John of the Cross

Journaling Space

"Therefore, we who are receiving the unshakable kingdom should have gratitude, with which we should offer worship pleasing to God in reverence and awe. For our God is a consuming fire."
—*Hebrews 12:28-29*

A NOTE TO THE READER
AMAZON REVIEWS

If you enjoyed this prayer journal, would you kindly post a short review of *Mary's Mantle Consecration: Prayer Journal* on Amazon.com? Your support will make a difference in the lives of others and help more people dive into their own souls in order to grow spiritually.

To leave a short review, go to Amazon.com and type in *Mary's Mantle Consecration: Prayer Journal*. Click on the book and scroll down the page. Next to customer reviews, click on "Write a customer review."

WOULD YOUR PARISH LIKE TO DO MARY'S MANTLE CONSECRATION?

IN THIS CRITICAL TIME IN THE CHURCH AND IN HUMAN HISTORY, ISN'T IT VITAL FOR CATHOLICS TO GROW IN VIRTUE, THE GIFTS OF THE HOLY SPIRIT, AND TO CONSECRATE THEIR LIVES TO THE BLESSED MOTHER?

Parishes around the nation are offering Mary's Mantle Consecration with great success and parishioners' gratitude. All it takes is a coordinator and a pastor's yes.
See www.MarysMantleConsecration.com for details.

OTHER BOOKS
BY CHRISTINE WATKINS

Available through
QueenofPeaceMedia.com and Amazon.com in
Print, E-Book, and Audiobook formats

Libros disponibles en español
www.queenofpeacemedia.com/libreria-catolica

EL AVISO
Testimonios y Profecías de la Iluminación de Conciencia

EL MANTO DE MARÍA
Una Consagración Mariana para Ayuda Celestial

EL MANTO DE MARÍA
Diario de Oración para la Consagración

TRANSFIGURADA
El Escape de las Drogas, de la Calle y de la Industria del Aborto,
de Patricia Sandoval

HOMBRES JUNTO A MARÍA
Así Vencieron Seis Hombres la Más Ardua Batalla
de Sus Vidas

OF MEN AND MARY
HOW SIX MEN WON THE GREATEST BATTLE OF THEIR LIVES

"Of Men and Mary is superb. The six life testimonies contained within it are miraculous, heroic, and truly inspiring."

—Fr. Gary Thomas

Pastor, exorcist, and subject of the book and movie, "The Rite."

(See www.queenofpeacemedia.com/of-men-and-mary

for the book trailer and to order)

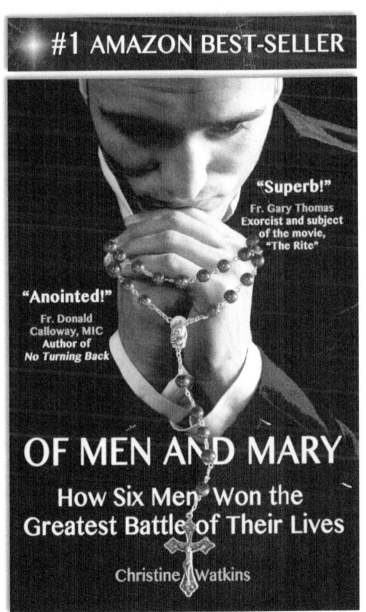

Turn these pages and you will find yourself surprisingly inspired by a murderer locked up in prison, a drug-using football player who dreamed of the pros, and a selfish, womanizing dare-devil who died and met God. You will root for a husband and father whose marriage was a battleground, a man searching desperately to belong, pulled by lust and illicit attractions, and an innocent lamb who lost, in a single moment, everyone he cared about most. And you will rejoice that their sins and their pasts were no obstacle for heaven.

TRANSFIGURED

PATRICIA SANDOVAL'S ESCAPE FROM DRUGS, HOMELESSNESS, AND THE BACK DOORS OF PLANNED PARENTHOOD

"The world, especially Catholics, need to read this story of redemption."
—Fr. Donald Calloway, MIC

**Archbishop Salvatore Cordileone & Bishop Michael C. Barber, SJ
Also available in Spanish: TRANSFIGURADA**

**(See www.queenofpeacemedia.com/transfigured
for the book trailer, the companion DVD, and to order)**

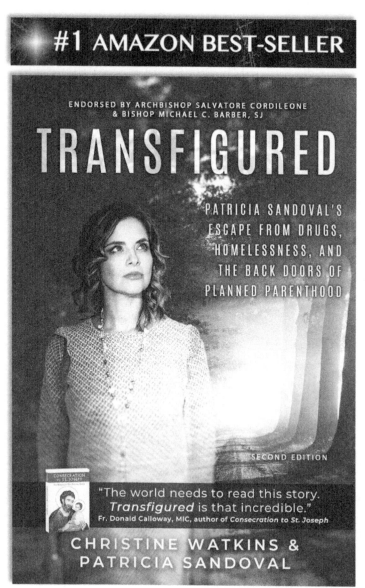

"Are you ready to read one of the most powerful conversion stories ever written? Seriously, are you? It's a bold and shocking claim, I admit. But the story you are about to have the pleasure of reading is so intense and brutally candid that I wouldn't be surprised if it brings you to tears multiple times and opens the door to an experience of mercy and healing. This story is made for the big screen, and I pray it makes it there someday. It's that incredible.

. . . What you are about to read is as raw, real, and riveting as a story can get. I couldn't put this book down!"

—Fr. Donald Calloway, MIC
Author of *No Turning Back*

FULL OF GRACE

MIRACULOUS STORIES OF HEALING AND CONVERSION THROUGH MARY'S INTERCESSION

"Christine Watkins's beautiful and touching collection of conversion stories are direct, honest, heart-rending, and miraculous."

—Wayne Weible

Author of *Medjugorje: The Message*

(See www.queenofpeacemedia.com/full-of-grace for the book trailer and to order)

In this riveting book, Christine Watkins tells her dramatic story of miraculous healing and conversion to Catholicism, along with the stories of five others: a homeless drug addict, an altar boy trapped by cocaine, a stripper, a lonely youth, and a modern-day hero.

Following each story is a message that Mary has given to the world. And for those eager to probe the deeper, reflective waters of discipleship—either alone or within a prayer group—a Scripture passage, prayerful reflection questions, and a spiritual exercise at the end of each chapter offer an opportunity to enliven our faith.

THE WARNING

TESTIMONIES AND PROPHECIES OF THE ILLUMINATION OF CONSCIENCE

Includes the riveting story of Marino Restrepo, hailed as a St. Paul for our century

(See **www.queenofpeacemedia.com/the-warning** for the book trailer and to order)

Authentic accounts of saints and mystics of the Church who have spoken of a day when we will all see our souls in the light of truth, and fascinating stories of those who have already experienced it for themselves.

"With His divine love, He will open the doors of hearts and illuminate all consciences. Every person will see himself in the burning fire of divine truth. It will be like a judgment in miniature."
—Our Lady to Fr. Stefano Gobbi
Founder of the Marian Movement of Priests

WINNING THE BATTLE FOR YOUR SOUL

JESUS' TEACHINGS THROUGH MARINO RESTREPO, A ST. PAUL FOR OUR CENTURY

Endorsed by Archbishop-Emeritus, Ramón C. Argüelles
"This book is an authentic jewel of God!"
—Internationally renowned author, María Vallejo-Nájera

(See <u>The Warning: Testimonies and Prophecies of the Illumination of Conscience</u> to read Marino's testimony)

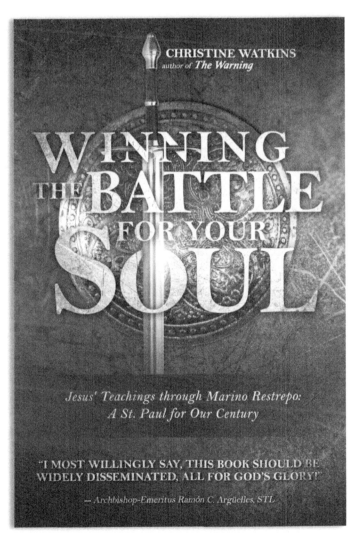

Marino Restrepo was a sinful man kidnapped for ransom by Colombian terrorists and dragged into the heart of the Amazon jungle. In the span of just one night, the Lord gave him an illumination of his conscience followed by an extraordinary infusion of divine knowledge. Today, Marino is hailed as one of the greatest evangelizers of our time.

In addition to giving talks around the world, Marino is the founder of the Church-approved apostolate, Pilgrims of Love.

This book contains some of the most extraordinary teachings that Jesus has given to the world through Marino Restrepo, teachings that will profoundly alter and inform the way you see your ancestry, your past, your purpose, and your future.

IN LOVE WITH TRUE LOVE
THE UNFORGETTABLE STORY OF SISTER NICOLINA

(See www.QueenofPeaceMedia.com and Amazon.com)

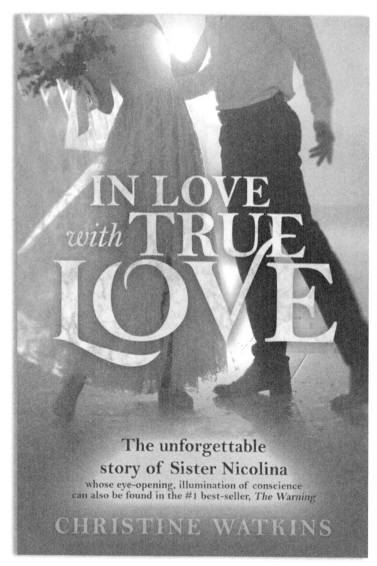

In this seemingly loveless world of ours, we might wonder if true love is attainable. Is it real, or is it perhaps a dancing illusion captured on Hollywood screens? And if this love dares to exist, does it satisfy as the poets say, or fade in our hearing like a passing whisper?

The souls are few who have discovered these answers, and one of them is Nicolina, a feisty, flirtatious girl who fell in love with the most romantic man in all of post-war Germany.

Little did they imagine the places where love would take them.

This enthralling real-life story is a glimpse into the grand secrets of true love—secrets that remain a conundrum to most, but are life, itself for a chosen few. Little-known chambers within the Heart of Love lie in hope to be discovered, and through this little book, may you, like Nicolina, enter their mystery and find life, too.

MARIE-JULIE JAHENNY
PROPHECIES AND PROTECTION
FOR THE END TIMES

(See www.QueenofPeaceMedia.com. Soon on Amazon.com)

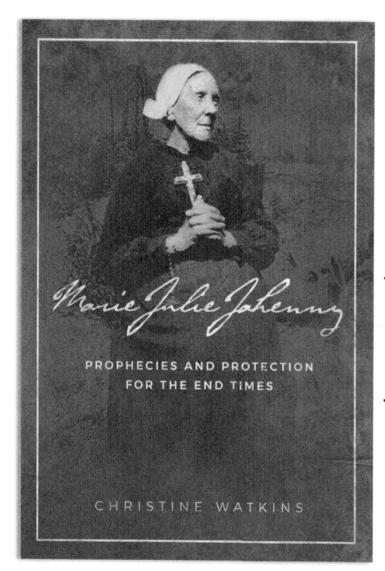

Marie-Julie Jahenny (1850-1941) is one of the most extraordinary mystics in the history of the Church. This humble peasant from devout parents in Britanny, France, received numerous visitations from heaven and lived with multiple wounds of the stigmata for most of her long life. Jahenny's selfless spirit endures as a gift to the Church, for she received knowledge of what lies on the horizon of our current era.

Jahenny was supported by her local bishop, Msgr. Fournier of Nantes, who said of her, "I see nothing but good."

In addition to Jahenny's special mission from the Lord to spread the love of the Cross, she was called to prepare the world for the coming chastisements, which precede and prepare the world for the glorious renewal of Christendom in the promised era of peace.

Through Marie-Julie, the Lord has given help, remedies, and protection for the times we now live in, and those soon to come. As Christ said to her on several occasions, "I want My people to be warned."

PURPLE SCAPULAR
OF BLESSING AND PROTECTION
FOR THE END TIMES

**Jesus and Mary have given this scapular to the world
for our times!**

Go to **www.queenofpeacemedia.com/product/purple-scapular-of-blessing-and-protection** to read about all of the incredible promises given to those who wear it in faith.

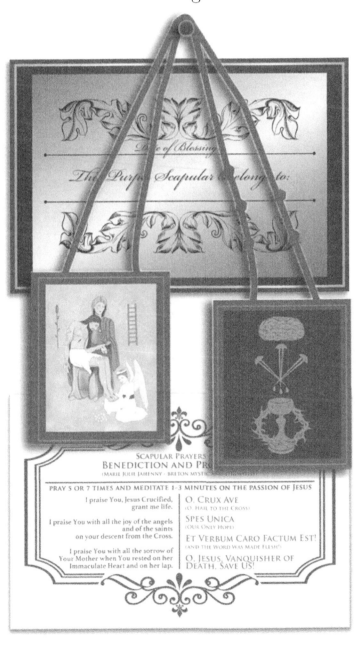

Our Lady's words to the mystic, stigmatist, and victim soul, Marie-Julie Jahenny: "My children, all souls, all people who possesses this scapular will see their family protected. Their home will also be protected, **foremost from fires**. . . for a long time my Son and I have had the desire to make known this scapular of benediction…

This first apparition of this scapular will be a new protection for the times of the chastisements, of the calamities, and the famines. All those who are clothed (with it) shall pass under the storms, the tempests, and the darkness. They will have light as if it were plain day. Such is the power of this unknown scapular. . ."

THE CROSS OF FORGIVENESS
FOR THE END TIMES

On July 20, 1882, Our Lord introduced THE CROSS OF FORGIVENESS to the world through the French mystic, Marie-Julie Jahenny. He indicated that He would like it made and worn by the faithful during the time of the chastisements. It is a cross signifying pardon, salvation, protection, and the calming of plagues.

Go to **www.queenofpeacemedia.com/product/cross-of-forgiveness** to read about all of the graces and protection given to those who wear it in faith.

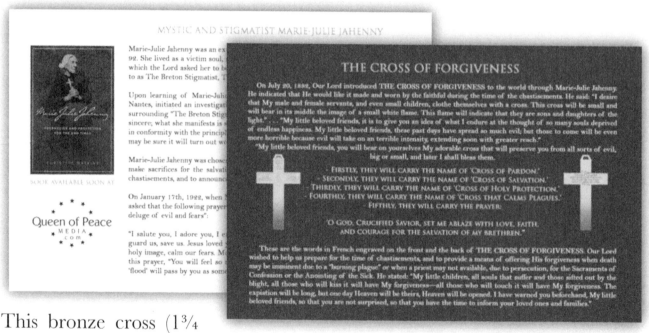

This bronze cross (1¾ inches tall and 1 inch wide) is a gift for our age and a future time when priests may not be readily available: "My little beloved friends, you will bear on yourselves My adorable cross that will preserve you from all sorts of evil, big or small, and later I shall bless them. . . My little children, all souls that suffer, and those sifted out by the blight, all those who will kiss it will have My forgiveness—all those who will touch it will have My forgiveness." The expiation will be long, but one day Heaven will be theirs, Heaven will be opened."

THE FLAME OF LOVE
THE SPIRITUAL DIARY
OF ELIZABETH KINDELMANN

(Go to www.QueenofPeaceMedia.com/flame-love-love-book-bundle) to receive the Flame of Love book bundle at cost!

Extraordinary graces of literally blinding Satan, and reaching heaven quickly are attached to the spiritual practices and promises in this spiritual classic. On August 2, 1962, Our Lady said these remarkable words to mystic and victim soul, Elizabeth Kindelmann:

"Since the Word became Flesh, I have never given such a great movement as the Flame of Love that comes to you now. Until now, there has been nothing that so blinds Satan."

ABOUT THE AUTHOR
CHRISTINE WATKINS

Christine Watkins is a popular Catholic author and keynote speaker. She was an anti-Catholic atheist about to die from her sins when she received a divine healing. Watkins brings to life stories of faith, including her own, and fascinating topics of Catholic spirituality. See www.ChristineWatkins.com.

Printed in Great Britain
by Amazon